Items should be returned on or before the last date shown below. Items not already requested by other borrowers may be renewed in person, in writing or by telephone. To renew, please quote the number on the barcode label. To renew online a PIN is required. This can be requested at your local library.
Renew online @ **www.dublincitypubliclibraries.ie**
Fines charged for overdue items will include postage incurred in recovery. Damage to or loss of items will be charged to the borrower.

Leabharlanna Poiblí Chathair Bhaile Átha Cliath
Dublin City Public Libraries

Baile Átha Cliath
Dublin City

Terenure Branch Tel: 4907035

Date Due	Date Due	Date Due
1 8 AUG 2018		

my first
CARD-MAKING
BOOK

35 easy-to-make cards
for every occasion for
children aged 7+

CICO **Kidz**

Published in 2017 by CICO Kidz

An imprint of Ryland Peters & Small Ltd

20–21 Jockey's Fields   341 E 116th St

London WC1R 4BW   New York, NY 10029

www.rylandpeters.com

10 9 8 7 6 5 4 3 2 1

ISBN: 978 1 78249 445 4

Printed in China

Series consultant: Susan Akass
Editor: Katie Hardwicke
Designer: Alison Fenton
Illustrator: Rachel Boulton
Character illustrations: Hannah George
Template illustrations: Stephen Dew

In-house editor: Dawn Bates
In-house designer: Fahema Khanam
Art director: Sally Powell
Production manager: Gordana Simakovic
Publishing manager: Penny Craig
Publisher: Cindy Richards

For photography credits, see page 112

Contents

Introduction

There's nothing nicer than receiving a handmade card, because you know that the person who sent it has really thought about you, not just rushed into a store to buy one. And there's also nothing more satisfying than making a beautiful card using your crafting skills—but sometimes it's hard to know where to start.

This book is full of exciting ideas to turn you into an expert card maker. It is divided into four chapters: Everyday Cards, Fun Cards, Festive Cards, and Special Occasions and you will find ideas for cards for all types of celebrations and festivals, from a birthday to Valentine's day, from a wedding to Christmas, and lots of everyday cards for birthdays or just to say thank you.

There are lots of crafting skills to try—cutting, sticking, tracing, sewing, printing, coloring, folding—with templates and step-by-step instructions to ensure that every project will be a success. You can use papercrafting skills to make origami rosettes for the card on page 48, or try

weaving paper to make an Easter basket on page 92. If you like sewing, show off your neat stitches on the cross-stitch card on page 23, or make a miniature dress to put on a coat hanger on page 50. There are 3-D options to choose from, too, from a pop-up Christmas tree on page 84 to fun popsicles on page 60. If you're feeling arty and creative, get stuck in with fingerprinting cute pups on page 70 or stenciling a lacy doily on page 100.

Before you begin, look through the techniques section, which explains all the basics from measuring, scoring, and folding a card, to making an envelope. You can also learn the simple stitches for the projects that involve sewing. Check the suggested list of materials so that you have what you need whenever there's a special occasion that needs a special card.

To help you plan your crafting we have graded all the projects with one, two, or three smiley faces—see opposite. Level one projects are the easiest and use very simple materials, level two are a little more complicated, and level three are the most challenging—but none of them are difficult, so get going and have fun!

Project levels

😊 ⚪ ⚪

Level 1
Quick and easy
projects that don't
require any adult help.

😊 😊 ⚪

Level 2
Projects that are a
little trickier and
may require some
adult help.

😊 😊 😊

Level 3
More challenging
projects that use
special materials or
require adult help.

Getting Started

It is useful to have these basic materials in your crafting kit, but for some projects you may need to find or buy some special materials. Check the "You will need" list for each project before you begin.

Basic equipment

Pencils
Ruler—a metal one is best for scoring
Pencil sharpener
Erasers
Felt-tipped pens
Acrylic paints
Thick and thin paintbrushes
Palette or plate for mixing paint
Water pot or jar
Glitter
Pair of sharp scissors with pointed ends
Glue stick
White (PVA) craft glue and spreader
Sticky tape
Masking tape
Sticky tack
Paper clips
Hole punch
Stapler

Paper and card

Ready-made card blanks and envelopes
White and colored paper
White and colored card
Colored tissue paper
Origami paper
Tracing paper
Doilies
Squared math paper
Paper towels

Recycling box

Greeting cards
Gift wrap
Cardboard packaging
Old newspapers and magazines (ask first before you cut them up!)
Wallpaper off-cuts
Envelopes and stamps

Sewing stash

Sewing needles and thread
Pins
Fabric scissors
Embroidery floss (thread) and needle
Yarn (wool)
Scraps of fabric and felt
Ribbons and braid
Buttons and beads

Craft Techniques

Copying templates

For some of the projects you need to copy a template from the back of the book (see pages 104–110), cut it out, and draw around it. You can trace some of the templates onto white paper or you can photocopy them onto paper or thin card. Some templates have to be enlarged and these ones will need to be photocopied—follow the percentage enlargement given with the template.

For some projects you will need to use tracing paper to transfer details from a template. This is how you use it.

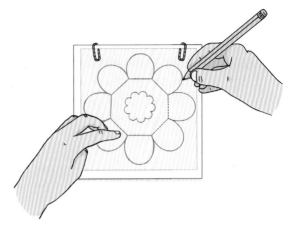

1 Place a sheet of tracing paper over the template and hold it in place with paper clips or masking tape. Trace the lines with a hard 4 (2H) pencil. Include inside details such as score lines.

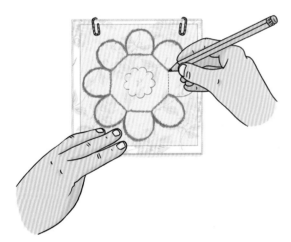

2 Turn the tracing paper over so that the back is facing you and neatly scribble over the lines with a softer pencil, such as a 2 (HB).

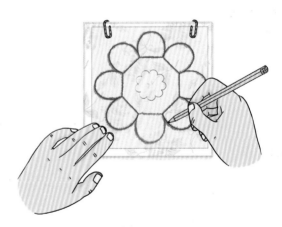

3 Turn the tracing paper over again so that the top is facing you and position it on your paper or card (use paper clips or masking tape to hold it in place). Carefully draw over the lines you made in Step 1 with the hard pencil, and then remove the tracing paper. This will transfer the pencil underneath to give you a nice, clear outline.

Making your own card blanks

You can buy greeting card blanks in craft stores or online, but it is also easy to make your own. You will need to learn to use a set square and do some careful measuring to ensure the corners of your cards are all right angles. Scoring the fold will make it look sharp and straight and professional.

You will need

....

Sheet of card

Ruler, pencil, and set square

Scissors

1 Decide on the size of your greeting card and then mark out a rectangle on the card, remembering to double the width. For example, for a folded card that is 5 in. (13 cm) wide and 7 in. (18 cm) tall, you need to measure a rectangle 10 in. (25 cm) wide and 7 in. (18 cm) tall. Use the corner of a sheet of card so you already have one right angle. Measure the width of the card from the corner along one edge and make a small mark with your pencil, then measure the height along the other edge and make another mark.

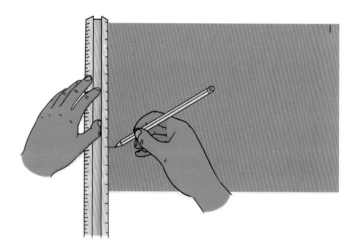

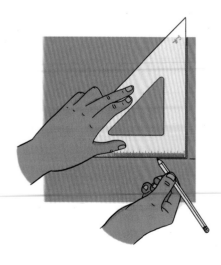

2 Line up a set square along one edge of the card with the right angle corner against the mark you have just made. Draw a line along the edge of the set square at right angles to the edge of the card. Repeat to draw the other sides of the rectangle. If you wish, you can take away the set square and line up your ruler so that you can make the line you have just drawn longer.

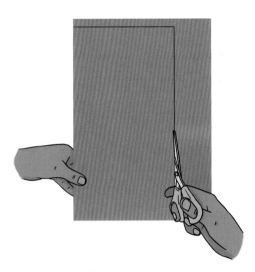

3 Join the end of the line with the mark on the other edge of the card to make a rectangle. Check that all your corners are right angles. Cut out carefully.

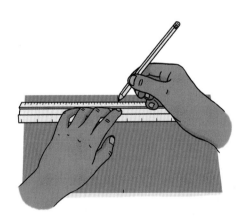

4 Measure along the width to find the center point on the top and mark this. Do the same on the bottom.

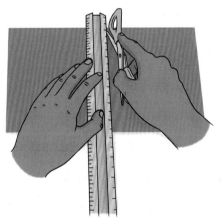

5 Place your ruler between the two marks and score firmly along it using the point of a pair of scissors (score means to mark a line along the cardboard using scissors, but not to cut all the way through). Now fold the card in half along the scored line, with the score on the outside of the card.

Making an envelope

When you've worked hard to create a special handmade card, you need something to keep it safe and looking good until it can be delivered. Using colored paper with a sticker or washi tape to seal it, here's how to make a simple, fun-looking envelope that you can adapt to any size of card.

You will need

....

Your finished card

Plain paper—the size depends on the size of the card

Glue stick

Washi tape, a sticker, or sticky tape (optional)

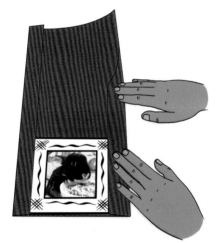

1 Put your card on a sheet of paper to check the size. Have the longer side of the card at the bottom of the paper—the paper should be at least 1 in. (2.5 cm) wider than the long side, and about two and a half times as long as the short side.

2 Center the card with one long edge lined up with the bottom of the paper. Fold in the long sides of the paper over the card edges on both sides. Crease the fold all the way up the paper.

3 Move the card up the paper, inside the flaps, so the bottom is where the top was before. Fold up the bottom of the paper, keeping the card inside and creasing the fold along the card, to make a pocket.

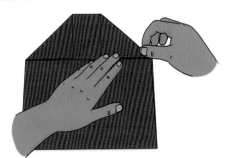

4 Fold the bottom piece back down and glue along the bottom half of the flaps below the crease. Fold up again and press the pocket edges together to stick them in place. Be careful not to get any glue on the card. (Gluing makes the envelope stronger but it will stay together without it, so you can miss this stage if you are not mailing your card.)

5 Take a corner of the top flap and fold it down to almost meet the pocket, making a diagonal crease. Do the same for the opposite side, then make a crease along the folded flap.

6 To seal your envelope, put a dab of glue on the underside of the flap, or use washi tape, sticky tape, or a fun sticker.

Making a bow

A bow is a lovely way to finish a card or notelet, so here are some simple instructions to help you to tie the perfect bow.

1 Make a loop in the ribbon and wrap the other end of the ribbon around, as if tying your shoelace.

2 Feed the wrapped ribbon through the hole, and tighten both loops to make a bow.

3 Adjust the ends until your bow is neat and symmetrical.

Sewing Techniques

Some of the cards use simple sewing or embroidery techniques to make something extra special. All the sewing techniques are easy to learn and do.

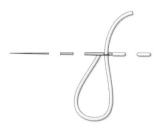

Threading a needle

Thread your needle with about 25 in. (65 cm) of thread or yarn (wool). Pull about 6 in. (15 cm) of the thread through the needle. Tie two knots on top of each other at the other end.

Running stitch

This makes a neat stitch when you are sewing two layers of fabric together. Secure the end of the thread with a few small stitches. Push the needle down through the fabric a little way along, then bring it back up through the fabric the same distance along. Repeat to form a row of equal stitches.

Backstitch

This is a very useful stitch, since it is strong and similar to the stitches used on a sewing machine. It makes a solid line of stitches.

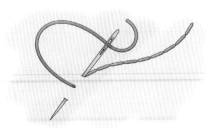

1 Start as if you were sewing running stitch. Sew one stitch and bring the needle back up to start the second stitch, bringing it up one stitch length ahead.

2 This time, instead of going forward, go back and push the needle through at the end of your first stitch.

3 Bring the needle out again a stitch length ahead. Keep going forward and back to make an even line of stitches with no gaps.

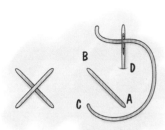

Cross stitch

To sew a single cross stitch, knot your thread, bring the needle up at A and down at B, then up at C and down at D. Secure the thread with a few stitches on the back.

Finishing stitching

It is important to finish off all your stitching so that it doesn't come undone. When you have finished stitching, sew a few tiny stitches over and over in the same place on the back of the fabric. Then trim off your thread.

Gathering

1 To gather a piece of fabric, knot your thread and begin with a few small stitches over and over in the same place on the fabric to hold the thread firmly so it won't pull through.

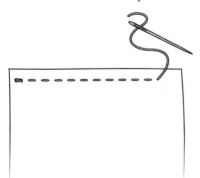

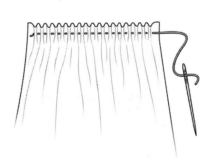

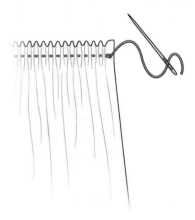

2 Now sew a line of running stitches—the smaller the stitches, the smaller the gathers you will make.

3 At the end, don't finish off; leave the thread loose. Pull the fabric back along the line of stitches so it gathers up into folds.

4 When it is the right size, secure the end of the thread with a few stitches over and over in the same place so the fabric can't come ungathered.

chapter 1
Everyday Cards

Felt Flower Card

Pretty flowers are a great way to say "thank you" or to celebrate a birthday or happy occasion. Make your flowers from bright, clashing colors of felt, and use a decorative sequin in the center to add a bit of sparkle.

You will need

Templates on page 105

Pencil, scissors, and ruler

Felt in bright colors (including green for the leaves)

White (PVA) craft glue

Two large sequins or foil shapes

Thin cream card

Colored paper

Glue stick

Narrow green ribbon

1 Copy the flower and leaf templates on page 105. Use the templates to cut out two large flowers and two small flowers in different colors of felt. Cut out three green felt leaves.

2 Using craft glue, stick one small flower to the center of one large flower, and then stick a sequin to the center. Make another flower with the remaining shapes. Allow to dry.

Tip
You can use different combinations of colors and sizes to make a range of cards, or use just one flower on a small square card.

3 Cut out a rectangle of cream card 6¼ x 12¼ in. (16 x 31 cm). Score down the center of the card and fold it in half.

4 Use the folded card as a template to lightly draw a rectangle 6 x 6¼ in. (15.5 x 16 cm) on the colored paper using a pencil, and cut it out neatly. Stick the colored paper onto the front of the cream card with a glue stick.

5 Glue the flowers onto the card with craft glue, positioning one higher than the other. Cut lengths of ribbon to make the flower stems and glue them onto the card, tucking the top ends underneath the felt. Finally, glue the leaves in place on the stems.

Say it with **FLOWERS!**

Blossom Hole-punch Card ●●○

Have you ever wondered what you could make with all the paper circles left inside a hole punch? Here's one idea— transform them into cherry blossom! This delicate card design is hidden behind two flaps, making it ideal for a special occasion like an anniversary or birthday.

You will need

....

Paper in pale pink, lilac, brown, and metallic green

Hole punch

Pencil, scissors, and ruler

White (PVA) craft glue and a small pot

Toothpick

Cream and pink card

Glue stick

Colored paper for the vase

1 Start by punching lots of holes in the pink and lilac papers. Collect the circles that are punched out. You will need about 54 circles in each color. Cut a strip of paper about ¼ in. (6 mm) wide in each flower colour and then cut the strips into squares— nine squares for each flower color.

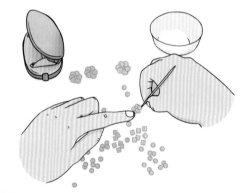

2 Use a toothpick to apply small dabs of glue to the backs of the circles and stick six circles of paper in one color onto a matching square of paper, overlapping each one slightly. This can be a bit fiddly. Try using another toothpick to move the circles around so you don't get glue on your fingers. Continue until you have nine flowers in each color.

Tip
A pretty alternative would be to make lots of the flower blossoms, then arrange and glue them into a circular shape to form a floral wreath.

3 Cut out a rectangle of cream card 5½ x 3¾ in. (14 x 9.5 cm). Cut out branch shapes from brown paper and stick them onto the cream card—draw the branch first, using a slight zigzag shape and finishing with a point at the top.

Take a **PEEK** inside!

4 Use the glue to stick the branches to the cream card, about a third of the way up to leave space for the vase. Arrange the branches so that their bases are close together. Now stick the flowers onto the branches, mixing up the colors, and glue in place with small dabs of craft glue applied with a toothpick.

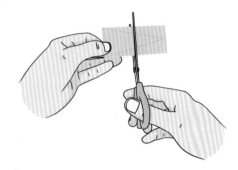

5 Cut a vase shape from brightly colored paper—you could draw a triangle by drawing lines from the top corners of a rectangle to the middle of the base, then cutting off the tip. Glue the vase in place over the ends of the branches.

6 Punch about 18 circles from the green paper and glue onto the branches between the flowers. Leave them slightly folded for a more three-dimensional look.

7 Cut a piece of bright pink card measuring 6 x 8 in. (15 x 20.5 cm). Measure and mark a faint line 2 in. (5 cm) in from each short side and score along this line. Fold along the score lines and stick the decorated panel onto the middle section using a glue stick.

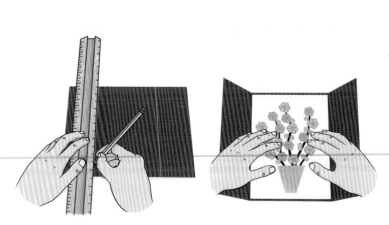

Cross-stitch Card

Here's a great way to practice your sewing skills and make something really special that your mother or grandmother will treasure—the finished card would look lovely in a frame. The gingham fabric provides you with a handy stitching grid, and fraying the fabric edges is good fun, too!

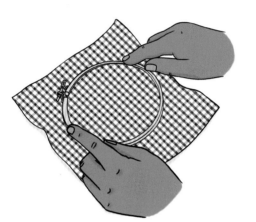

1 Separate the two rings of the embroidery hoop. Place the gingham fabric over the smaller, inner ring and then replace the outer ring, stretching the fabric until it is tight and smooth and tightening the outer ring to hold it in place.

You will need

Embroidery hoop or frame

12 x 12 in. (30 x 30 cm) piece of gingham fabric

Air soluble marker pen

Embroidery needle

Embroidery floss (thread) in a contrasting color

Iron

Scissors

Pin

White (PVA) craft glue

Card blank

Button, ¾ in. (2 cm) diameter

2 Use the marker pen to mark out a square with sides that are each 11 gingham squares long, in the middle of the frame (the marks will disappear after you have finished stitching). Use a little dot inside each check to mark the square. Then mark another square just inside this one and a third square inside this. This will leave a blank square in the middle for the button.

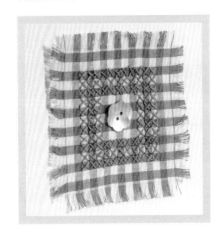

Stitches or KISSES?

3 Thread your needle with a length of embroidery floss and begin to work cross stitches (see page 15) across the marked square, pushing your needle into the corners of the gingham checks to keep the stitches even. Turn the embroidery hoop as you work the square. When you've finished, secure your thread with a few stitches on the back.

4 Remove the embroidery hoop and ask an adult to help you to press the back of the fabric flat using a hot iron.

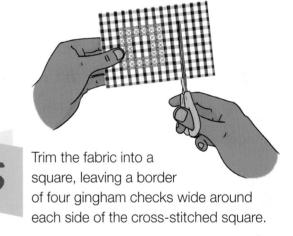

5 Trim the fabric into a square, leaving a border of four gingham checks wide around each side of the cross-stitched square.

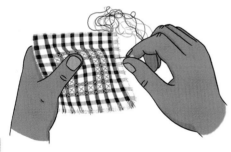

6 Start pulling the loose threads of the gingham gently away from the fabric to create a frayed edge. Use the point of a pin to pull away the threads until you have frayed the width of two gingham checks on each side of the fabric square.

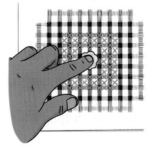

7 Add a little glue to the back of the fabric and stick the gingham square to the center of the card. Press firmly to stick it in place. Finish your card by gluing a pretty button to the center of the cross-stitched square.

Flower Stamp Card

This card uses the shapes cut out with a decorative craft punch to make a repeating pattern. We've used a flower punch but there are lots of designs to choose from in craft stores, from hearts and butterflies to snowflakes and boats.

You will need

Pencil, scissors, and ruler

Thin card in cream, lime green, and blue

Decorative craft punch

Coordinating colored papers (about five different colors)

Glue stick

1 Cut out a rectangle of cream card 5 x 7¼ in. (12.5 x 18.5 cm) to use as your background.

2 Position the craft punch on the edge of a piece of colored paper and push down to cut out the shape. Move the punch along the edge to cut out more shapes. Repeat on the other pieces of paper until you have about 24 flowers in total, in different colors.

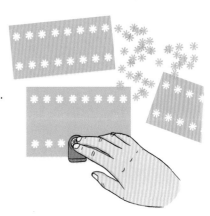

Tip
Make smaller versions to use as gift labels, or decorate envelopes to match the card.

3 Arrange the flowers on the cream card—you can either place them randomly or make a regular pattern of six lines of four flowers, making sure that no flowers of the same color are placed next to each other. Stick them in place, using a glue stick.

STAMP OUT and stick

4 Cut out a rectangle of lime green card 5¼ x 7¾ in. (13.5 x 19.5 cm). Glue the decorated cream card on top so that there is a small even border of green all the way around.

5 Cut out a rectangle of blue card 12 x 8½ in. (30.5 x 22 cm). Score down the center of the card and fold it in half. Stick the flower card on the front of the folded card, making sure there is an even blue border all around it.

Op Art

Op art is a style of art that often uses geometric shapes, like circles and squares, to produce different effects, or optical illusions. This cool greeting card would be perfect for an older brother, or as a Father's Day card, using their favorite colors or the colors of their soccer team.

You will need

Thick white paper or card

Pencil, ruler, and scissors

Tissue paper in three different colors

Roll of tape, small lid, or button, about 1 in. (2.5 cm) in diameter to draw around

Glue stick

1 Measure and cut out a rectangle from the paper or card 4¾ x 9½ in. (12 x 24 cm). Then score down the center of the card and fold it in half to make a square card.

2 Cut out about 20 tissue paper squares 1½ x 1½ in. (4 x 4 cm). There will be a grid of 9 squares in your card design, but because you will be layering the tissue paper you will need about 20 in total to produce a great effect. Use a ruler to mark off strips on the tissue paper 1½ in. (4 cm) wide, and then cut out squares along the strip.

3 Now, using your lid or roll of tape to draw around, cut out a selection of different colored tissue paper circles to fit in the squares. Again, cut out about 20.

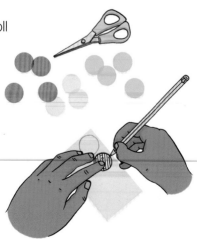

Tip

For this project, you can layer your tissue paper to make different hues and varying tones. The hue is the color and the tone means how light or dark that color is.

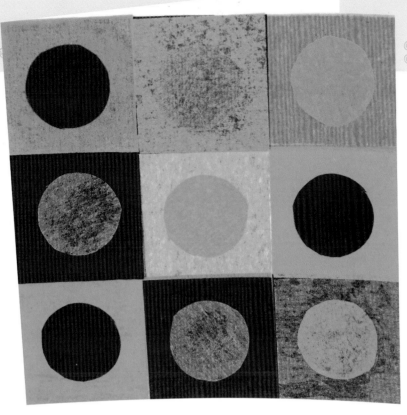

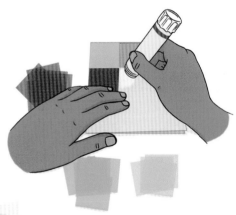

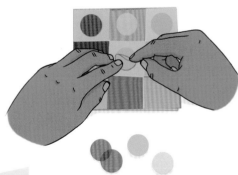

4 Start to stick your squares onto the front of the card in a grid pattern. Tissue paper can be tricky to glue because it tears easily—try gluing the card rather than the paper for the first layer. Add more layers to build up the colors, experimenting with different combinations before you stick.

5 Next, add your tissue paper circles, carefully gluing them in place and using different color combinations to create an optical effect. Add lots of layers. Let dry completely.

It's all an **ILLUSION** ...

Ribbon Bouquet Card ●○○

Is it coming up to Mother's Day or is your sister getting married? Make a truly special card for a special occasion, using ribbon embroidery.

You will need

Template on page 106

Piece of thin cream card

Paper and pencil

Sticky tape

Narrow ribbon in pretty flower colors

Embroidery needle

Scissors and ruler

Pale green embroidery floss (thread)

8½ x 11-in. (A4) piece of thicker colored card

Glue stick

1 Cut out a rectangle of cream card 6¾ x 4¼ in. (17 x 11 cm). Photocopy or trace the design for the embroidery on page 106. You'll need a sunny day for the next stage. Use a couple of pieces of sticky tape to tape the design pattern onto a window. Hold the cream card over the top. You should be able to see the design through the card. Lightly trace over the design in pencil.

2 Cut a length of ribbon and thread it through the needle. Tie a double knot in the end. Starting from the back, bring the needle through the card in the position of the first flower. Stitch the flower petals over the pencil lines.

3 The flowers have different color centers and petals so, before you finish off, take the needle underneath the card to the center of one of the other flowers and stitch two stitches. Finish on the back with a knot. Now thread your needle with another color ribbon and stitch a second flower and a different center. Stitch the last flower and the last center in the third color. Trim the ends of the ribbon on the back of the card.

4 Thread the needle with green embroidery floss and tie a knot at the end. Starting from the back of the card, embroider lines of small back stitches (see page 14) along the flower stems.

5 Thread the needle with a 7-in. (18-cm) length of pink ribbon. Push it through from the front of the card to the back and through to the front again, without a knot, and tie into a small bow (see page 13). Trim the ends of the ribbon to the same length.

6 Score the piece of colored card across the center and fold it in half. If you want a cut-out frame for your card, place the embroidered card carefully in the center of the inside front of the folded card and draw around it. Draw another rectangle with sides about ½ in. (1 cm) in from the sides of the first one. Ask an adult to cut this rectangle out using a craft knife.

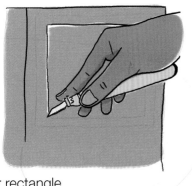

7 Glue around the inside of the frame and push the embroidered card against it. You may need to add a little sticky tape on the inside to hold it firm.

Flower Fairy Card

When you press flowers you capture a little piece of summer and turn it into something fragile and beautiful. Use flowers and leaves from your garden (ask permission first), press them between the pages of a heavy book and use them to create these magical flower fairies.

You will need

Template on page 106

Fresh flowers and leaves

Flower press or a few heavy books (heavy catalogs are good for this)

White and colored paper

Blotting paper (optional)

Cream and colored card

Pencil, scissors, and ruler

Glue stick

1 Collect colorful fresh flowers and small leaves. Find a place in your room where you can leave a pile of books that won't be moved for a week! Find a few large, heavy books that are all about the same size. (If you have your own flower press, you won't need the books.)

2 Open one book and lay a piece of white paper—or blotting paper—over one of the pages. Arrange the flowers on the paper so they don't touch or overlap. Lay another piece of paper on top of the flowers and close the book.

3 Pile a few more books on top for extra weight. Leave for about a week.

4 Using the fairy template on page 106, cut out a fairy shape without the hair, then draw around it on plain colored paper and cut it out.

5 Stick the fairy onto a piece of cream card about 6 x 4 in. (15 x 10 cm). Use the template to cut out the fairy's hair from colored paper and stick in place.

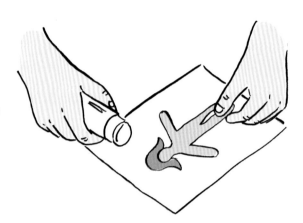

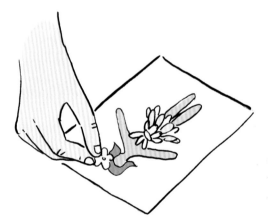

6 Lift off the books, open the paper, and carefully remove the flowers. Arrange them on the paper fairy to make a pretty dress and hat. When you are happy with the arrangement, carefully lift each flower or petal and dab some glue onto the paper below it. Press the petal or flower down gently to stick it in place.

7 Cut a 7 x 5-in. (17.5 x 12.5-cm) piece of colored card, score down the center, and fold it in half. Glue the flower fairy onto the front, leaving an even border of colored card all the way around.

Fold-out Petal Card

Open up this pretty 3-D card and find a secret message hidden inside! This card looks really impressive but the skills you need to make it are simply careful cutting out and paper folding.

1 Cut out two squares of thin patterned card, each 5½ x 5½ in. (14 x 14 cm). Stick them together back to back, so that the pattern appears on both sides.

You will need

Templates on page 110

Pencil, scissors, and ruler

Thin patterned card, about 6 x 12 in. (15 x 30 cm)

Glue stick

Tracing paper

Paper clips

Patterned paper in 2 different designs

Thin white card, about 6 x 12 in. (15 x 30 cm)

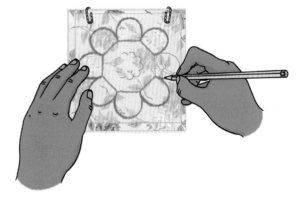

2 Trace the large flower template on page 110 and transfer (see page 9) all the outside lines and the dashed lines to one side of the card square. Use paper clips to hold the tracing paper in place when you trace from the template and when you transfer the tracing to the card. Don't trace over the inner flower yet.

3 Cut around the outline of the flower shape. A good technique is to turn the card not the scissors and to always cut from the outside of the card toward the center of the flower. Make sure to cut right down to the dashed lines so that the petals are separated.

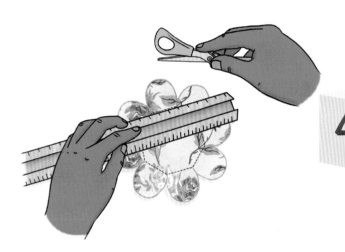

4 Gently score along the base of each petal along the dashed line, and fold them upward.

5 Now trace the small flower template on page 110 and transfer the shape to one of the patterned papers. Cut out the shape and stick it in the center of the folding flower. Fold down the scored petals, overlapping each one and tucking the last petal underneath the first to secure it.

6 Cut out a piece of white card 5½ x 11 in. (14 x 28 cm) and a piece of patterned paper the same size. Glue the patterned paper to the card. Mark the center of the patterned card with a light pencil line.

7 Use the tracing of the large flower again, placing it on the right-hand side of the patterned card with the ends of two of the petals about ¼ in. (6 mm) over the center line (use paper clips to hold it in place). This is so that when you cut away the flower shape, the front of the card is still attached to the back section by these two petals. Trace over the large flower shape only.

8 Score down the center of the patterned card following the pencil line you made in step 6, and fold the card in half. Cut out the flower shape through both layers of the card. Be very careful not to cut the card where it is folded so that the back and front are still attached together by the ends of the two petals.

9 Glue the folded flower section onto the center of the flower card.

Surprise, SURPRISE!

Button Nest Card

On this pretty card, tiny buttons are used to make a robin's nest. Pearl buttons can be expensive, but look out for them in thrift stores (charity shops). Use printed and patterned papers for the bird and leaves—try magazines or gift wrap.

You will need

Templates on page 110

18 x 12 in. (45 x 30 cm) thin blue card

Pencil, scissors, and ruler

Selection of small buttons

Sewing needle and thread

Sticky tape

Sheets of printed and colored paper, including red for the breast

Glue stick

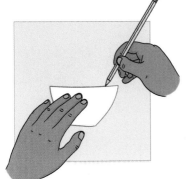

1 Trace the templates on page 110 onto thin paper (or photocopy them) and cut them out. Cut out a piece of card 5½ x 5½ in. (14 x 14 cm). Draw around the nest template with a very light pencil line to mark out the area for the nest.

2 Sew on the buttons for the nest. Thread the needle and knot the end. Hold a button in position and bring the needle up through the card and one hole of the button, and then down through the other hole. Repeat a couple of times to secure the button, then sew on the next button without fastening off the thread. Try not to bend the card as you sew. If you run out of thread, knot the end and start another piece. Sew enough buttons to fill the outline of the nest. Secure the loose ends of thread with pieces of sticky tape.

3 Draw around the remaining templates for the robin, leaves, and twigs on different areas of the printed paper, making sure that you use red for the breast. Cut out the shapes.

4 Glue the robin, breast, twigs, and leaves in position on the card. You can use a circular piece of paper or a tiny button for the robin's eye.

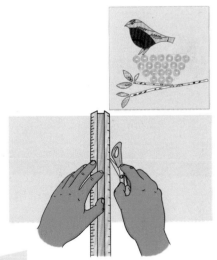

5 Cut out a rectangle of card 5½ x 11 in. (14 x 28 cm). Score down the center of the card and fold it in half. Stick the robin card onto the front of the card.

Raffia Card

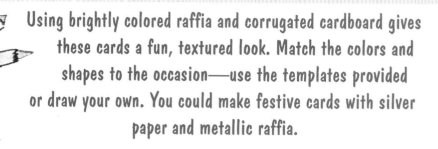

Using brightly colored raffia and corrugated cardboard gives these cards a fun, textured look. Match the colors and shapes to the occasion—use the templates provided or draw your own. You could make festive cards with silver paper and metallic raffia.

You will need

Template on page 110

Pencil, scrap paper, and scissors

Thin corrugated cardboard

Rotary hole punch (optional)

Sticky tack or modeling clay

Colored raffia

Embroidery needle

Sticky tape

Ruler

White (PVA) craft glue

Tip

Make miniature cards as gift labels using a simple circle motif.

1 Photocopy or trace the template on page 110 and cut out the shape. Lay the corrugated cardboard bumpy side down and draw around the template. Cut out the shape with scissors.

2 On the bumpy side of the heart, mark the position for the holes by pushing your pencil point through the marks on the template. Punch out the holes either using a sharp pencil or the smallest setting on a rotary hole punch tool. If you use a pencil, put the cardboard on top of a piece of sticky tack to protect your table. Always push the pencil from the bumpy side down to make a neat hole. Make the center hole bigger as lots of raffia will need to go through it.

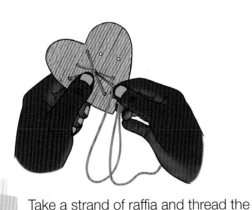

3 Take a strand of raffia and thread the needle. Make a knot in the raffia and bring it up through the center hole, down through one of the outer holes, and back up through the center. Continue until you have made a star shape and used all the holes. Secure the ends of the raffia on the back with sticky tape.

4 Cut out a rectangle of colored card measuring 11 x 5½ in. (28 x 12.75 cm). Score down the center of the card and fold it in half. Glue the woven corrugated card shape to the front of the card, holding it until it is stuck in place.

Wallpaper Notelet

This card uses leftover wallpaper to make a notelet that is perfect as a thank-you card, or you could make a set and give them as a gift. If you don't have any wallpaper, look out for bargains at the home supply store—they may let you have old sample books—or use sheets of gift wrap instead.

You will need

Pencil, scissors, and ruler

Scrap of old wallpaper or gift wrap

Piece of thin card

White (PVA) craft glue

Hole punch

Ribbon

1 Choose a pretty part of the wallpaper and cut out a rectangle 5¼ x 3½ in. (13.5 x 9 cm). Cut a rectangle of the thin card measuring 11½ x 3½ in. (29 x 9 cm).

2 Score down the center of the card and fold it in half.

3 Use a thin layer of craft glue to stick the piece of wallpaper to the right-hand end of the piece of card, so that the outside edges match.

4 Make holes for the ribbon. With the card opened out, use the hole punch to make a hole at the bottom of the card on the strip of plain card, to the right of the fold. Then do the same at the top.

5 Cut a piece of ribbon about 17 in. (44 cm) long. Thread it through the holes and tie in a bow on the front (see page 13), trimming the ends at an angle.

A pretty way to say **THANK YOU**

Patchwork Card

The robin on this fun card is ready to deliver the mail! Make a patchwork background for him with old labels, bits of packaging, stamps, envelopes, paper bags, old comics, and math paper. Write a message to go inside the tiny envelope!

You will need

Template on page 106

Thin white card

Pencil, scissors, and ruler

Scraps of labels, stamps, envelopes, and math paper

Scraps of brown and red paper

Hole punch

Glue stick

1 Cut a rectangle of white card 6 x 12 in. (15 x 30 cm). Score down the center of the card, and then fold it in half. Cover the front of the card with the scraps of paper you have gathered together to make a patchwork.

2 Copy the templates on page 106 and cut out the three sections of the bird. We used plain brown for the whole robin, red for the breast, and a scrap from an envelope for the wing. Punch out a hole for the eye.

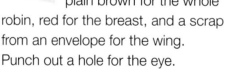

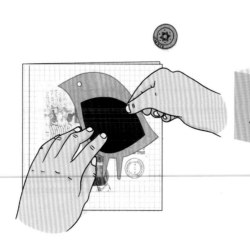

3 Position the bird about ½ in. (1 cm) in from the right edge and glue in place, adding the red breast and wing on top.

4 To make the mini envelope in the bird's mouth, cut out the envelope shape from the template on page 106 on colored paper. Fold in the two side flaps and glue them on the top. Fold the bottom section of the envelope up over them and hold down until it sticks.

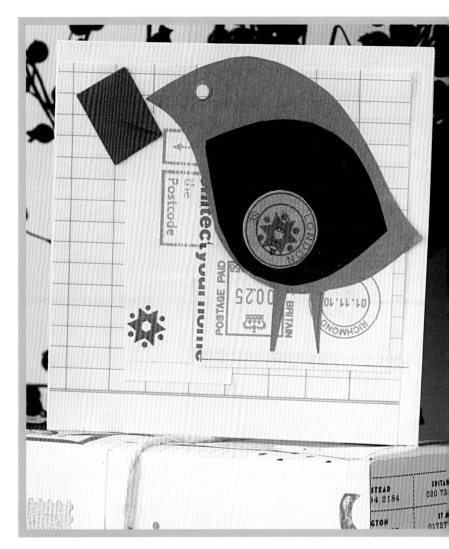

5 Fold over the top flap of the envelope, but don't stick this part down; you need to keep it open so that you can place a little message inside! Glue the envelope to the card next to the bird's mouth.

Tip
You can make matching gift wrap, too—first wrap your gift in brown paper, then make a patchwork from lots of scraps of paper over the top.

chapter 2

Fun Cards

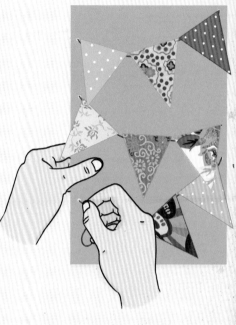

Rosette Card

If you have ever made a paper fan, you'll know how to make these impressive 3-D cards, which make perfect thank-you cards or even party invites. The concertina folding is quite relaxing and you'll soon have a production line going!

You will need

Coordinating patterned papers in similar colors, such as origami paper

Pencil, scissors, and ruler

Stapler and staples

White (PVA) craft glue

Paper clips (optional)

Plain colored paper for background

Thin cream card

Glue stick

1 Cut out 4 pieces of patterned paper 2½ x 3½ in. (6 x 9 cm). Begin folding the paper from one end into a concertina shape, making each fold about ¼ in. (6 mm) wide. Start with one fold, creasing the paper with your fingertip to get a neat, crisp edge. Turn the paper over and make another fold the same width. Keep turning, folding, and creasing until you reach the end.

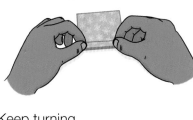

2 Staple the folded paper together horizontally across the middle. Cut the ends into a rounded shape using scissors.

3 Open out the rosette and glue the edges together to form a complete circle. Hold the glued edges tightly in place until dry—you could use a paper clip to hold them together. Make a further two or three rosettes in this way.

Tip
Hand delivery is a good idea for these 3-D cards to prevent the rosettes getting crushed in the mail.

4 Cut a rectangle of paper 7½ x 5 in. (19 x 13 cm) and a rectangle of cream card 5½ x 16 in. (14 x 40.5 cm). Score down the center of the card and fold in half.

5 Glue the plain paper rectangle onto the front of the cream card using a glue stick, making sure you have an even border all the way round. Now, using a small dab of craft glue, stick on the rosettes in your chosen arrangement. Hold them in place as they dry.

Coat Hanger Card

This cute design—a little fabric dress hung on a tiny coat hanger— is perfect to send to a special friend who enjoys crafting and sewing. By making it, you'll get to use different skills and you can mix and match the fabric and the background card to fit with your friend's favorite colors.

You will need

Template on page 109

Scraps of pretty fabric

Needle and thread

Pencil, scissors, and ruler

Pins

Thin silver jewelry wire

Pliers

Thin card in cream and pink

Glue stick

White (PVA) craft glue

Thin ribbon or ready-made craft bow

1 Photocopy or trace the template on page 109 for the top of the dress and the coat hanger. Cut them out and cut a paper rectangle for the skirt about 2 x 2¾ in. (5 x 7 cm). Pin the templates onto the fabric and cut out with scissors, or draw around the template on the wrong side (the back) of the fabric, and cut out.

2 Thread a needle and knot the end. Sew small running stitches along the top of the skirt rectangle (on a long side) and gather it up (see page 15) so that it measures 1½ in. (4 cm) wide. Finish with a few small stitches over and over in the same place to hold the gathers. Use craft glue to stick the skirt to the top of the dress. Leave until the glue dries completely.

A pretty dress for a special FRIEND

3 Take a 10-in. (25.5-cm) length of silver wire. Fold it in half and hold the folded end with the pliers, leaving a loop. Twist the two ends of wire around themselves until they are twisted together all the way down.

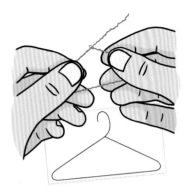

4 Using the coat hanger template shape on page 109 as a guide, carefully bend the wire to form a coat hanger, pushing the ends through the loop and bending them into a hook shape at the top. Trim the ends of the wire neatly (you may need to ask an adult to help you).

5 On the wrong side of the fabric, put a dab of craft glue on each shoulder of the dress and fold them over the top wires of the coat hanger. Press firmly to stick in position.

6 Cut a rectangle of pink card 6¼ x 10 in. (16 x 25.5 cm). Score down the center of the card and fold it in half. Cut a rectangle of cream card 4 x 5½ in. (11 x 14 cm) and glue it onto the pink card, making sure that there is an even border around it.

Tip
Choose a fabric with a small print in a retro design to match the old-fashioned style of the dress.

7 Put small dabs of craft glue on the back of the dress and glue it onto the card. Finish the dress with a small bow, using about 6 in. (15 cm) of ribbon (see page 13), or use a ready-made bow. Attach it to the dress with craft glue.

Mini Bunting Card

Bunting means it's party time! These cards are great for any celebration and you can change the colors to suit the occasion, such as red hearts for Valentine's Day and soft pastels to celebrate the birth of a baby. Collect scraps of gift wrap or patterned paper and use colored twine to match your color scheme.

1 Cut out a piece of white card 10 x 8 in. (25.5 x 20 cm) and a piece of colored paper 5 x 8 in. (12.5 x 20 cm).

2 Trace the template on page 110 and cut out the triangle. Draw around it onto some scrap cardboard and cut it out to use as a template. Draw around this template onto scraps of colored paper to make the bunting flags. Cut out nine flags in different papers.

You will need

....

Template on page 110

Pencil, scissors, and ruler

Piece of thin white card

Thick colored paper

Tracing paper

Small piece of scrap card

Small pieces of bright colored paper

Modeling clay or sticky tack

Thin colored twine, string, or yarn (wool)

Glue stick

Needle

Masking tape

Tip
Tie lengths of bunting around gifts for a fun look.

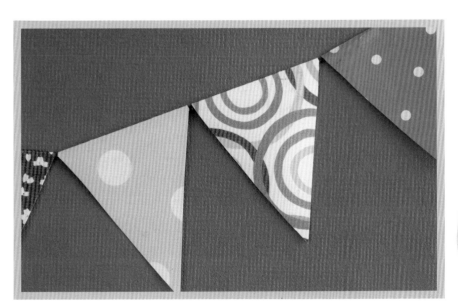

3 Cut three pieces of thin, colored twine about 6 in. (15 cm) long. Glue along the triangle of paper on the wrong side. Then fold it over the piece of thin twine, at least 1 in. (2.5 cm) away from the end, and glue down. Repeat until you have three flags in a row. Make two more strings of three flags.

4 Position the piece of colored paper with the short edges at the top and bottom (portrait format). Before you make the holes, place a piece of modeling clay or sticky tack beneath where you are going to push the needle through to protect your surface. Use the needle to make a small hole in the top right-hand corner and then another hole about 1 in. (2.5 cm) down from the top on the left-hand side. Make four more holes, two on the right and two on the left, so that the bunting will zigzag down the card.

5 Thread the end of one piece of twine through the top right hole and hold it in place on the back with a small piece of tape. Thread the other end through on the left and secure. Repeat with the remaining strings. If you have trouble pushing the twine through the hole, wrap a small piece of sticky tape around the ends of the twine to stiffen it.

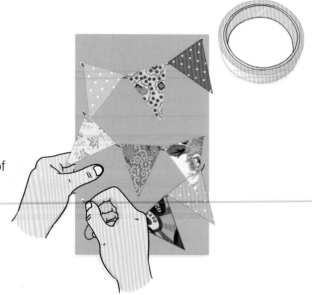

6 Score the rectangle of white card and fold in half. Glue the back of the colored paper and stick it to the front of the card so that the bunting hangs down.

Fly the **FLAGS!**

Owl Card

These funky cards use scraps of bright paper in contrasting colors and patterns to make super-cute owls, with 3-D beaks. Keep a supply of leftover paper from other projects so that you have everything to hand when an owl card is required!

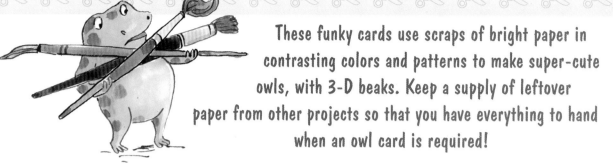

You will need

Template on page 108

Pencil

White paper

Thin white card, about 6 x 12 in. (15 x 30 cm)

Scissors and ruler

Patterned and solid-colored paper

Glue stick

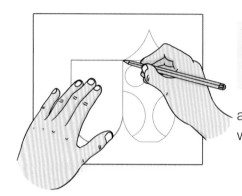

1 Photocopy the template on page 108 or trace it onto white paper and cut it out (see page 9). Draw around the owl shape onto the white card, and cut out.

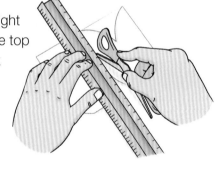

2 Score where there are straight lines on the template (at the top of the card where the beak folds over and the center where the card folds in half). Fold along the score lines to make a card with the beak folded down on the outside.

3 Using the owl shape and beak from the template, draw around the body (the front of the card shape) on patterned paper. Then cut out the eye and wing shapes from the template, and draw around these on different colored papers. Finally, draw around the beak on a solid color. Cut out all the pieces.

4 Stick the body in place then add the wings and eyes. Next, glue the beak onto the folded-down flap.

Tip
For the eyes, try to find scraps of paper with circular designs— flowers look great.

These cards are a HOOT!

Finger Puppet Card

A greetings card and a present all in one, these finger-puppet greeting cards are great for younger brothers, sisters, or cousins. You can make the characters shown here or use the basic pattern and invent your own heroes and villains.

You will need

Templates on page 104

Paper

Pencil and scissors

Flesh-colored felt

Scraps of felt in different colors

White (PVA) craft glue

Pins

Yarn (wool) for hair

Embroidery flosses (threads) and a needle

Thin card in pastel colors

Adhesive pads

1 Copy the templates on page 104 and then cut out the pieces you need for your finger puppet character. Fold the flesh-colored felt in half and pin the basic puppet shape to it. Cut it out to give you two puppet shapes. Pin the clothes patterns to a single layer of felt and cut them out.

2 Glue the clothes to the front of the puppet, using craft glue. Cut some short lengths of yarn and glue in place as the hair. Let them dry. Leave the hat off until later.

3 Cut a length of black, brown, or blue embroidery floss and tie a knot in the end. Starting from the wrong side, embroider a cross stitch for each eye (see page 15). Finish on the wrong side with a knot. Now thread the needle with red floss, tie a knot, and embroider another cross stitch for the mouth. Finish off on the wrong side with another knot.

4 Pin the front of the puppet to the back. Thread the needle with embroidery floss to match your puppet's clothes and tie a knot. Starting with the knot on the inside of the puppet, stitch the two sides together using small running stitches (see page 14). Finish off with another knot inside the puppet. Now glue on the hat.

5 Cut a piece of card 6 x 8¼ in. (15 x 21 cm), score down the center, and fold it in half. Using felt and the templates from page 104, cut out the background shapes for the card.

6 Stick the shapes onto the card using craft glue and let them dry. Attach the finger puppet to the card with an adhesive pad.

Time for a STORY

Popsicle Card

A bright, 3-D popsicle card is perfect for a summer birthday or a beach party. Use brightly colored scraps of fabric to make these popsicles look good enough to eat!

You will need

....

Templates on page 105

Pencil and ruler

Pointed scissors

Pins

Bright fabrics such as gingham check and polka dots

Light brown paper for the popsicle sticks

Thin card cream card

Thin pastel-colored card

White (PVA) craft glue

Glue stick

1 Copy the popsicle and stick templates on page 105. Cut the shapes out and pin the popsicle to the fabric. Use sharp fabric scissors to cut out three shapes from different patterns. Draw around the stick template on brown paper and cut out three sticks.

2 Cut a rectangle of cream card 8½ x 6 in. (22 x 15.25 cm). Draw a faint pencil line horizontally along the center of the card. This will be a guide to where to place the popsicle shapes and where the card folds.

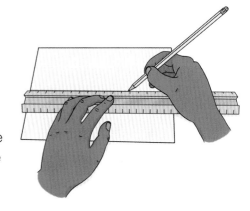

3 Apply white (PVA) craft glue to the back of the fabric popsicle shapes. Stick one in the middle of the card with its base about 1½ in. (4 cm) below the central pencil line. Stick the other two shapes on either side, spacing them equally and making sure the bases line up. Using the glue stick, attach the popsicle sticks.

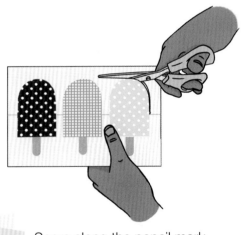

4 Score along the pencil mark between the popsicles and at either end of the card. Use pointed scissors to push through the card and cut carefully around the top of the popsicles, above the center line.

POP-UP popsicles!

5 Cut an 8½ x 6¼-in. (22 x 16-cm) rectangle of pastel card. As before, measure and score a line along the center of the card and fold. Glue the inside of the cream card with glue stick (but do not glue the tops of the popsicles above the center line) and place over the top of the colored card. Fold the card over where the center line is drawn to display the card with the lollipops standing up.

Frame Card

○○○

Frame a photo or picture with this stylish card design. Print your photo in black and white for a cool, sophisticated look, or use a colorful artwork. You can enlarge or decrease the size of the template to fit your own designs, making this a really unique card for any occasion.

You will need

A photocopier or scanner and printer

Template on page 109

Thin white card, suitable for use in a photocopier or printer

Pencil, scissors, and ruler

Glue stick

Photograph or picture

1 Photocopy the template on page 109 onto white card and cut it out.
To cut the center of the frame, make a small hole with your scissors, then cut to the inside edge.

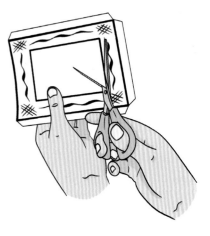

2 Score the fold lines along each of the three flaps and fold the flaps under to the wrong side (the back).

3 Cut out a rectangle of card 10 x 3¾ in. (25.5 x 9.5 cm). Measure and score at the halfway point across the rectangle and fold the card in half.

Tip
Copy the frame onto red card and insert a Christmas family photo for a festive greeting card.

4 Place the frame right side down on the table and place the front of the card over it. Glue along the flaps of the frame, then fold them over to the inside of the card and press them into position. Let the glue dry.

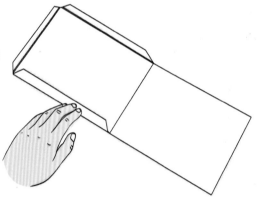

5 Take your photograph or picture and check the size against the card, trimming it to fit if you need to. Slide your photograph in through the open edge.

You've been **FRAMED!**

Russian Doll Card

This card is inspired by traditional wooden nesting dolls from Russia. After a clever bit of tracing and cutting, the concertina-folded card is quite simple to finish with some folksy gift wrap and colored paper. You can either use the same paper for each doll or mix up the patterns.

You will need

Template on page 106

Tracing paper

Pencil

12 x 5 in. (30 x 12.5 cm) thin white card

Scissors

Scraps of a variety of patterned papers

Glue stick

Scraps of plain colored paper for the faces

Craft knife or fine felt-tipped pen

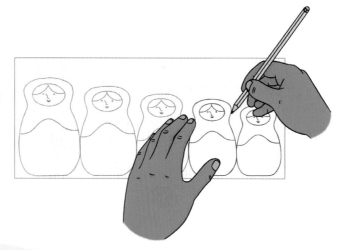

1 Copy the doll template at full size (100%) and then four more times, reducing the size by 8% each time—92%, 84%, 76%, and 68%. Line them up from biggest to smallest, then trace the templates onto one piece of tracing paper. Make sure that each doll is butted right up alongside the next in line so that they are touching on one side.

2 Transfer (see page 9) the outline of the row of dolls onto the piece of thin card. Cut out the entire row, keeping the dolls joined together.

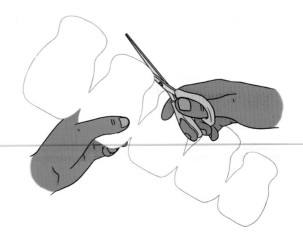

3 Use the individual shapes on the templates to cut out the different size body shapes from patterned paper. Once you have traced the body, cut out the head scarf template and cut out pieces from the solid-colored paper.

PRETTY maids all in a row

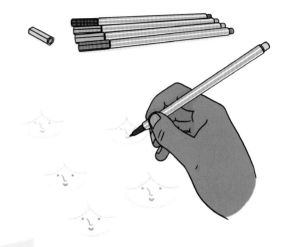

4 Use glue stick to stick on the matching body shape, and then the head scarf, onto each doll in the row.

5 Trace the oval for each face onto white paper. Use the templates to draw the faces, then color them in with a fine felt-tipped pen.

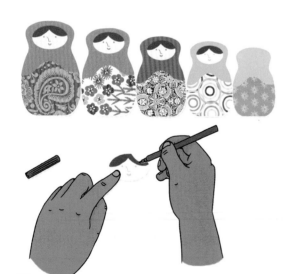

6 Color in the hair on the face section, or cut out the hair shape for each doll and stick it down. Stick each face onto its matching body.

7 Score down the join where each doll is attached to the next in the row. Fold the dolls back and forward to make a concertina shape.

Handbag Card

All girls love a stylish handbag and these fabulous cards look as good as anything you can buy! Using patterned gift wrap and some pretty ribbon, you'll soon be making these for all your friends and family—simply lift the flap to write your greeting inside the bag.

You will need

Templates on page 107

Pencil and ruler

Pointed scissors

Thin, pale colored card

Patterned gift wrap

Glue stick

Colored tissue paper

Ribbon, about
1 in. (2.5 cm) wide

White (PVA) craft glue

Small adhesive pads

1 Copy the templates on page 107 and cut out. Draw around the bag shape and the front flap pieces on colored card and cut out. Mark the score lines in pencil. To cut the handle, make a small hole with the points of your scissors and cut around the inner edge.

Tip
You can replace the wide ribbon with thin velvet ribbon, and tie a little bow to stick to the front of the card.

2 Use the glue to stick the cardboard shapes to the back of the giftwrap (score lines facing up so you can still see them). Then cut around the card carefully and cut out the center of the handle.

3 Cut out another handle shape from the gift wrap and stick it to the other side of the handle so both sides of the handle are covered in matching paper.

4 Score along the score line on the plain card side of the bag piece and fold it neatly in half. Open it up again. Now score along the score line at the top of the flap piece and make a sharp fold along this line. Use craft glue to glue along the folded strip and stick the flap just underneath the handle. Hold in place until firmly stuck.

5 Cut a long strip of tissue paper about 16 x 1 in. (40.5 x 2.5 cm). Apply a line of glue to the underside of the flap and stick the tissue paper to it, pleating it as you go, so that half of the pleats show over the edge. To pleat, fold the paper to the side for the first pleat, then fold again so the fold of the second pleat lines up with the back of the first pleat. Keep folding like this all along the flap. Press down firmly.

6 Fold the flap down over the bag. Cut a length of ribbon to match the width of the flap and glue it to the front just a little way above the pleated tissue paper. To make the flat bow, cut an 8-in. (20.5-cm) length of ribbon. Make it into a loop with the join at the center of the back and glue the two ends down.

7 Now cut a 2½-in. (6-cm) length of ribbon and glue it over the middle of the loop, holding it in place at the back with craft glue. Stick this onto the band of ribbon.

8 Stick an adhesive pad to the outside of the bag and match it up with a pad on the inside of the flap to close the card.

RIBBONS and BOWS!

Fingerprint Pups

Why not paint a special portrait of your pet as a birthday card? Remember, simple shapes work the best. Look at your pet—it may have a round face and an oblong body, or curly hair and a square-shaped body. Do rough drawings first until you are happy with the shape, then get messy!

You will need

....

Card

Ruler

Scissors

Pencil

Poster paint

Old saucer

Black marker pen

Soft eraser

1 To make a sausage dog card, cut a piece of card 8 x 10¼ in. (20 x 26 cm). Fold it in half, so that you have a card that measures 4 x 10¼ in. (10 x 26 cm).

2 With the fold at the top, draw a long oblong shape lightly in pencil on one side of the card. Make sure you leave space all around to add the head, legs, and tail. You don't need to use a ruler—a rough shape will add to the charm!

Tip
You can make dogs in all shapes and sizes. Try making a pink poodle with a pompom hairstyle!

Who can resist these adorable PUPS?

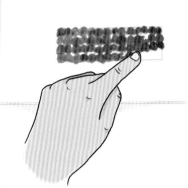

3 Mix up some paint on an old saucer. Use your fingertip to make dots and fill in the oblong shape. Go right up to the pencil line; it doesn't matter if you go over it. Let the paint dry.

4 Use a pencil to draw in a head, the feet, and, of course, a waggy tail! When you are happy with your pencil lines, go over them with a black pen. Use a soft eraser to rub out any remaining pencil lines you can see.

chapter 3
Festive Cards

Glitter Star Card

A card that doesn't need an envelope—an exciting, glittery surprise to arrive in the mail at the house of your best friend, aunt, or grandma! Just fold the flaps, seal with a glittery dot, and your card is ready to be sent.

You will need

Template on page 105

White paper

Pencil and scissors

Scrap paper

Small coin

White (PVA) craft glue

Glitter in a similar color to the card

Thin colored card

Ruler

Silver paper

Glue stick

1 Trace the star template on page 105 onto the white paper and cut it out carefully. On a scrap of spare paper, draw around a small coin and cut this circle out too.

2 Cover the star and the circle with a thin layer of craft glue. Put them on some scrap paper and sprinkle over the glitter until they are covered. Shake any glitter that has not stuck off onto the scrap paper and pour it back into the pot. Let the shapes dry.

3 Cut out a piece of card 4¾ x 10 in. (12 x 24 cm). Measure 2½ in. (6 cm) from each short side in two places, join the marks with a ruler and score gently with the point of the scissors. Fold the card along the score lines so that the two sides fold into the center.

4 Measure a 4 x 4-in. (10 x 10-cm) square of silver paper. Cut it out and stick it centrally inside the card using the glue stick.

5 Use some more craft glue to stick the star into the center of the square.

6 Write your greeting inside one of the side flaps. Close the flaps over the star.

7 Using the glue stick, place the glitter circle across the two flaps to hold them closed. The circle will pull off easily to open the card. Write the name and address on the back of the card and it is ready for mailing.

Color-in Christmas Card

This project is a card and a gift in one! You get to do all the fun coloring, cutting, and gluing to make a festive greeting card and when you take the Santa out of his chimney, and pop your fingers through the holes, he becomes a funny little finger puppet!

You will need

Templates on page 108

White card

Pencil and pointed scissors

Ruler

Dark blue card

Felt-tipped pens or colored pencils

Glue stick

Stick-on diamanté gems

1 Copy the Santa and chimney templates on page 108 onto white card and cut them out. Cut a rectangle of white card 6 x 8 in. (15 x 20 cm), score down the center, and fold in half. Cut two rectangles of dark blue card, one measuring 4 x 6 in. (10 x 15 cm) and one measuring 2 x 4 in. (5 x 10 cm).

2 Color in your Santa and chimney using red, black, brown, and light brown felt-tipped pens or colored pencils. Cut out the finger holes in your Santa—push the point of your scissors in to make a small hole and then carefully cut out the inner edge of the finger holes, turning the paper to help you cut the circles.

3 Open the white card and use a glue stick to glue the larger piece of dark blue card onto the right-hand side inside. To make a pocket for your Santa puppet, add a line of glue along three sides of the smaller piece and stick it to the bottom of the card on the left-hand side, leaving one long edge unstuck for the top of the pocket.

4 Stick the chimney to the front of the card. Use scissors to cut across the front of the card from just above the chimney until you get to the fold. Now cut down the center fold, from the top of the card, to remove the top front of the card.

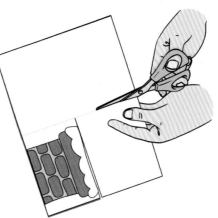

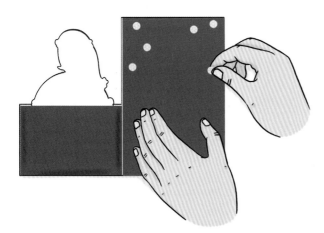

5 Finally, pop the Santa puppet into the inner pocket so that he faces out, and stick a few diamanté gems onto the dark blue background for falling snowflakes. (If you haven't got any gems, you could use a silver pen or star stickers instead.)

Cut-out Bauble Card

Have fun choosing bright and sparkly papers to use for these cut-out bauble cards. They have a funky, modern look that will be a great addition to the festive decorations.

You will need

Template on page 107

Colored card in three contrasting colors

Pencil, scissors, and ruler

Sheets of paper in bright and metallic colors

Glue stick

1 Copy the template on page 107. Draw around the bauble shape onto colored card— something bright or maybe silver or gold—and cut it out.

2 Now cut out the inner ovals from the template, draw around these onto shiny paper, and cut out. Finally, cut the circles from the center of the oval templates, draw around these onto a contrasting shiny paper, and cut them out.

3 Cut a piece of card 8 x 8 in. (21 x 21 cm). Score down the center of the card and fold in half. Cut a piece of different colored paper 4¼ x 8¼ in. (10.5 x 21 cm) and stick it to the front of the card.

BRILLIANT baubles!

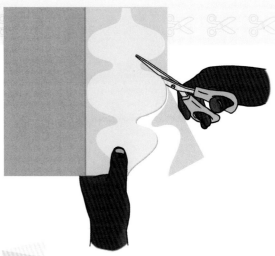

4 Stick the bauble shape on to the card with the top edge of the bauble in the center of the top edge of the card. Open the card and carefully cut around the right-hand edge of the bauble shape.

5 Following the template guide, glue the cut-out oval shapes in position on the bauble and then glue the circles on top.

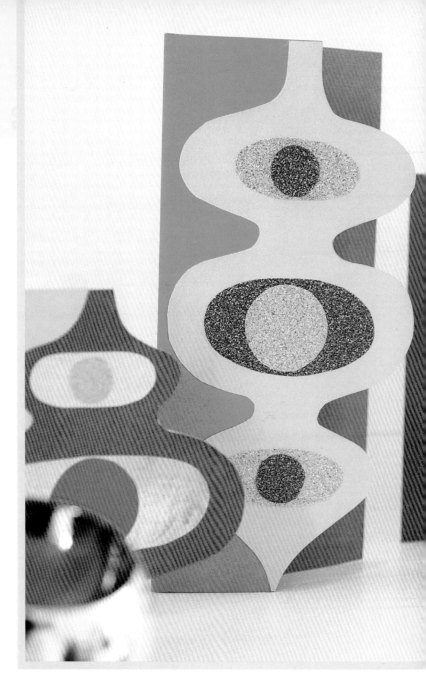

Tip
Why not make matching tags in bauble shapes to give your gifts that extra-special personal touch?

Christmas Stocking Card ●●○

Think how great a collection of these cards would look hanging along a mantelpiece or shelf, a different design for each member of your family. When making these cards, there's lots of crafting fun to be had with spots and ruffles, ribbon and braid.

You will need

....

Template on page 105

Pencil and scissors

Thin card in white and red

Red and white circular stickers

Red and white patterned gift wrap

Glue stick

Ruler

Red crepe paper

Needle and red thread

White (PVA) craft glue

A selection of braids and ribbons

Hole punch

1 Copy the stocking template on page 105. Draw around the template on red and white card, making one stocking for each member of your family. Cut out the stocking shapes.

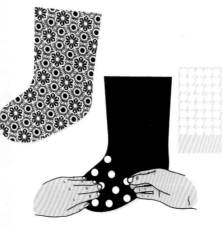

2 For the spotted stockings, stick circular stickers randomly all over one side of the card stocking. For a patterned design, draw around the template onto patterned paper or gift wrap, and cut out. Glue this onto a plain card stocking with glue stick.

3 To make cuffs for the top of the stockings, draw around the top of the template on a different colored card and then draw a line straight across about 2 in. (5 cm) from the top to make a rectangle. Cut it out.

4 To make a ruffle, cut a 12 x 1-in. (30.5 x 2.5-cm) strip of crepe paper. Stitch along one long edge with running stitch (see page 14), securing the thread with a knot at the start. As you sew, gently pull the paper along the thread, gathering it up into pleats until it measures 4¼ in. (11 cm). Finish with a few stitches over and over. Spread craft glue along the bottom of a cuff and glue the crepe paper ruffle along this.

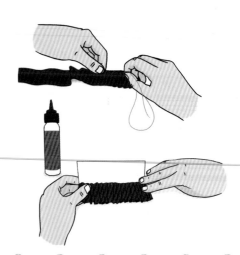

5 Decorate the cuffs with lengths of ribbon and braid. Cut each piece about 1 in. (2.5 cm) longer than the width of the cuffs. Lay the strips of ribbon over the card, moving them around until you are happy with the arrangement. Glue the ribbons onto the card, leaving ½ in. (1.5 cm) overhanging at each end. To save mess, don't apply glue to these overhanging ends. Turn the cuff over, fold down the ends, and glue them in place. Glue the cuff to the top of the stocking. Add a ribbon bow, if you like (see page 13).

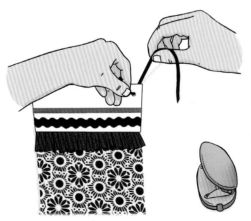

6 Using one end of the hole punch, make a hole in the top corner of each stocking. Cut a 6-in. (15-cm) length of thin red ribbon and thread it through the hole. Tie a knot in the ribbon and trim the ends to neaten them. Write your greeting on the reverse.

Embroidered Snowflake Card ☺☺☺

The sewing on this card is very simple. Finish it with pretty decorations—buttons if you have them, or stick-on jewels, sequins, or stars. If you are going to make more than one card, use different colors of card and floss. We've used eight points here, but you could make this with six points, like real snowflakes.

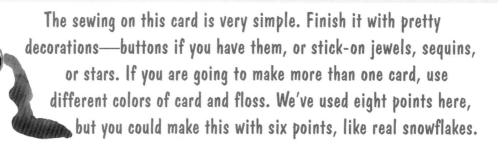

You will need

Template on page 108

Tracing paper, 6 x 6 in. (15 x 15 cm) square

Pencil

Square card blank, about 6 x 6 in. (15 x 15 cm)

A piece of thick corrugated card from a cardboard carton (for piercing holes)

Masking tape

Large needle

Thimble (optional)

Embroidery needle

Embroidery floss (thread)

Scissors

8 miniature buttons, ¼ in. (6 mm) diameter (or stick-on jewels or sequins)

White (PVA) craft glue

Miniature velvet bow (or 4 in./ 10 cm of narrow velvet ribbon to make one)

1 Trace the snowflake design from the template on page 108 onto the square of tracing paper. Open out the card and lay it flat on the corrugated cardboard. Stick the tracing paper to the front (the right-hand side) using small pieces of masking tape around the edges. Now use the large needle to make holes through the center, through the ends of all the lines and through all the places where lines meet, pushing it right through the tracing paper and card and into the cardboard below. Remove the tracing paper.

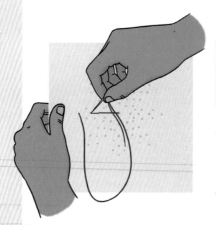

2 Thread the embroidery needle with the floss and knot the end. Insert the needle from the back of the card to the front through the center. Work along one arm of the snowflake. Take it down through the next hole and up through the next. You will then have a gap, so go back through the hole before and then make a long stitch underneath to come up through the next new hole. This is backstitch (see page 14).

Tip
You may find it easier to use a thimble to protect your fingers when marking the holes in step 1.

3 When you have completed a straight line, stitch the single lines on the edges, bringing the needle up on the outer end and taking it down  through a hole you have already used in the long line. Sew the pairs of stitches back down to the center and then start a new arm. You will see the snowflake design begin to appear as you embroider. Make sure that you haven't left any gaps.

4 You will probably need more than one piece of thread to complete the design. When you finish a piece, remove the needle and use a piece of masking tape to secure the thread end on the back.

5 Place the card on the table and use a little masking tape to hold it closed and flat. Stick the eight miniature buttons at the end of each point of the snowflake and attach a tiny bow to the center—either use a ready-made bow or make your own (see page 13. Let the glue dry completely.

Pop-up Tree Card ● ○ ○

These 3-D cards are really simple to make and you'll have lots of fun decorating them with paints, glitter, or stickers. Write your greeting on the back, then carefully fold and take to the mail.

You will need

Template on page 105

Thin green card

Scissors and pencil

Paints

Fine paintbrush

Glitter and white (PVA) craft glue (optional)

1 Copy the Christmas tree template on page 105 and cut it out using scissors. Place the template onto a folded piece of card. Draw around the template in pencil, lining up the long edge of the Christmas tree template exactly with the fold of the paper. Note there is an edge on the bottom branch that you mustn't cut.

2 Using scissors, carefully cut around the tree shape, making sure you do not cut through the section at the bottom of the tree marked on the template. This keeps the pop-up tree attached to the card itself.

3 Open out the card carefully and push the Christmas tree shape forward so that it stands away from the folded card to create a 3-D effect. Now you can see how important the uncut side sections are, because they keep the tree shape attached to the card.

Tip
For a pretty edge to the card, cut around it with decorative edge scissors, available from craft stores.

4 Lay the card flat again and use a fine paintbrush to add colorful "baubles" on the tree. Paint small gift boxes scattered around the base to finish the card. You can add glitter if you'd like, for a sparkly festive effect.

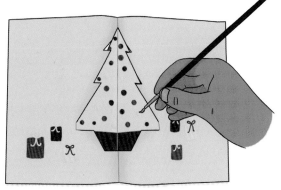

CREATE 3-D tree magic!

chapter 4
Special Occasions

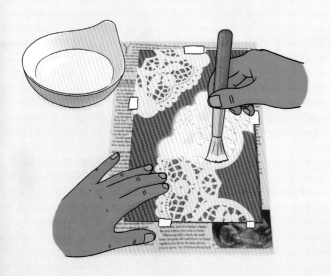

Heart Print Card

This simple card is made with a potato print cut using a heart-shaped cookie cutter. It makes the perfect Valentine's card and once you have cut the potato it is easy to print lots of cards to say "I love you!" to all the special people in your life.

You will need

Pink or white card

Pencil, scissors, and ruler

Decorative-edge scissors (optional)

Medium-sized potato

Cutting board

Sharp knife

Heart-shaped cookie cutter

Paper towel

Thick poster paint

Saucer to hold the paint

Scrap paper

White (PVA) craft glue

Paper flowers

1 Cut an 8-in. (20-cm) square of white card. Score down the center of the card and fold in half. If you have some decorative scissors, cut around the card, cutting through both sides together so they match.

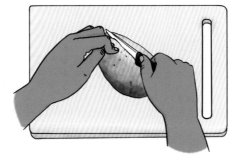

2 Put the potato on a cutting board and ask an adult to help you to cut the potato in half with the knife, making sure that the surface of the potato is as flat as possible.

3 Place the cookie cutter on the cutting board with the sharp cutting edge facing upward. Press the potato down on the cutter so that it is pushed in about halfway. Ask an adult to help you cut away the potato around the shape using a sharp knife. Remove the cutter.

HEARTS and FLOWERS...

4 If the cut surface of the potato is wet, blot it on a piece of paper towel. Pour some paint onto a saucer and dip the potato in the paint. Make sure the whole shape is covered, but take care not to sink the shape too deep into the paint.

5 Experiment with printing on some scrap paper to find out the best technique before you print on the card. Press the potato shape down firmly onto the paper. Make sure that the whole design prints clearly, by using a gentle rocking motion, without lifting it from the paper or sliding it around. This will help to apply the paint evenly. When you are confident about printing, make two prints on the card, one below the other, and let the paint dry.

6 When the paint has dried, glue a paper rose to the top of each heart to finish. Let the glue dry completely before writing in the card.

Easter Egg Card

Eggs and Easter go together so these very simple,
pretty egg cards with their ribbons and bows are
perfect for a special Easter greeting.

You will need

Template on page 105

Pencil, scissors, and ruler

Thin card in cream and pastel colors

Spotted gift wrap in two different colors

Glue stick

Chunky ricrac braid

Pastel-colored ribbon

White (PVA) craft glue

1 Copy the egg template on page 105 and cut it out. Draw around the template onto pastel colored card and cut out neatly—turn the card not the scissors on the curved edges.

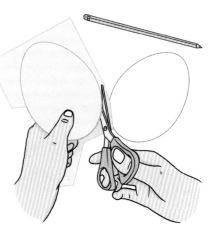

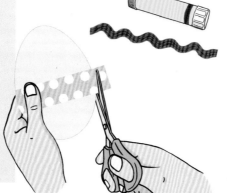

2 Cut a strip of spotted paper 1¼ x 3¾ in. (3 x 9.5 cm). Apply glue stick to the back and stick it across the egg. Trim the ends to match the curve of the egg.

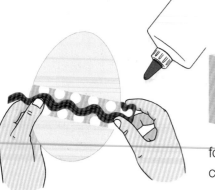

3 Cut a 4¼-in. (11-cm) length of ricrac, run a line of craft glue right along it, and glue it across the spotted strip, folding over the ends to the back of the card and gluing in place. Allow to dry.

Tip

Use a large egg on each card or smaller ones in a line for a variation. Use a photocopier to reduce the template size if you want to do this.

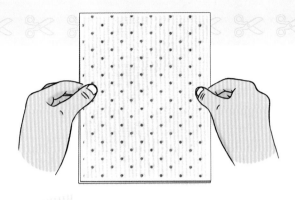

4 Cut out a rectangle 4¾ x 6¼ in. (12 x 16 cm) from the other spotted paper. Cut out a rectangle of cream card 13½ x 5½ in. (34 x 13.5 cm). Score down the center of the card and fold in half. With the fold of the card at the top, not the side, glue the spotted paper to the front of the card making sure that there is an even border all around it.

5 Glue the egg to the center of the card. Cut a 12-in. (30.5-cm) length of ribbon and tie in a bow (see page 13). Glue the bow to the top of the egg with a dab of craft glue.

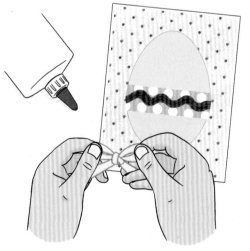

Make your card **EGGS-TRA** special!

Easter Basket Card  ● ○ ○

The pretty basket on this card is made by weaving paper. Fill the basket with eggs cut from pastel papers in varying sizes, and add a strip of tissue paper "grass" for a card worthy of any Easter egg hunt.

You will need

....

Templates on page 104

Pencil, scissors, and ruler

Thin card in lavender, cream, and pale yellow

Glue stick

Scrap paper

Decorative-edge scissors (optional)

Pastel-colored papers for the eggs

Green tissue paper

11-in. (28-cm) length of pink ribbon, 1 in. (2.5 cm) wide

1 Measure and cut out nine strips of yellow card, each ½ x 4½ in. (1 x 10.5 cm). Measure and cut out six strips of yellow card, each ¼ x 3½ in. (5 mm x 9 cm).

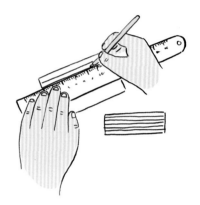

2 Lay one of the wider strips horizontally on the table. Stick one end of all six thin strips to this with the glue stick so that the strips lie vertically, ½ in. (15 mm) apart.

3 Glue the end of a wide strip to the thin strip on the far left, making sure that it butts up to the strip along the top. Weave the rest of the strip through the vertical strips. Glue the other end of this wide strip to the underside of the vertical strip on the far right.

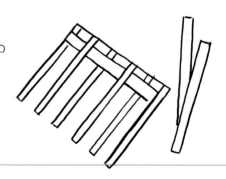

Pretty SPRINGTIME colors

easter basket card **93**

4 Glue another wide strip to the underside of the vertical strip on the far left, butting it up to the previous strip again, and weave as before. Glue the end in place on the far right. Continue until all the thick strips have been woven, remembering to alternate going under and over the strips to form a basket weave. Make sure that all the ends are firmly glued in place.

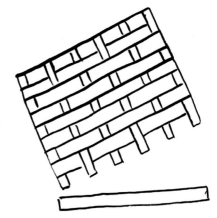

5 Apply glue stick to the back of the woven panel and stick it onto some scrap paper. Using the basket template on page 104, draw the basket onto the woven panel and cut out.

6 Dab glue onto any ends of the strips that are not stuck down. If you have some decorative-edge scissors, cut out a strip of yellow card about ½ in. (1 cm) wide and long enough to trim the top and bottom of the basket. Glue it in place. Don't worry about this stage if you don't have decorative-edge scissors.

7 Cut out a handle, using the template on page 104. Use your decorative-edge scissors if you have some, otherwise use normal scissors.

8 Cut a 6 x 8½-in. (15.25 x 22-cm) rectangle of cream card.

9 Using the egg template on page 104, cut out about seven paper eggs in a variety of colors.

10 Glue the basket handle onto the cream card and press down firmly. Arrange the paper eggs on the card and glue them in place.

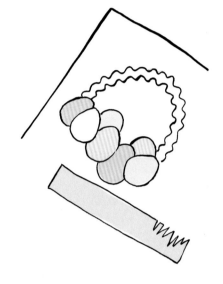

11 Cut a strip of green tissue paper 4½ in. (11 cm) long and ¾ in. (2 cm) wide. Make "V"-shaped snips about two-thirds through the width of the tissue paper to look like grass, and stick along the bottom of the eggs.

12 Glue the basket shape in place, making sure that it is well stuck down. Tie a neat bow with the ribbon (see page 13) and stick it onto the top of the basket.

13 Cut a 9 x 12½-in. (23 x 32-cm) rectangle of lavender card. Score down the center and fold it in half. Glue the basket card onto this to finish the card.

Tip
You can replace the handle and decorative strip of paper with a piece of ricrac braid or pretty ribbon, if you don't have decorative-edge scissors.

Picasso Postcard

These postcards are inspired by one of the most well-known artists of all time, Pablo Picasso. Before starting your collage, do some sketches and pick out things that would make good shapes, such as lots of windows in a tall building or pots and plants.

You will need

Scraps of colored paper

A sketch of your chosen subject

Thin white card

Ruler

Large and small scissors

Glue stick or white (PVA) craft glue

Colored pencils

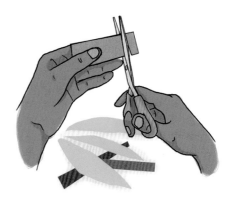

1 Gather together some scraps of colored paper. You can use bits of magazines and newspapers or packaging. Using one of your sketches as a guide, cut out some shapes of the buildings or landscape.

2 Cut out some postcards of thin white card measuring about 4 x 6 in. (10 x 15cm).

 3 Stick down your cut-out shapes onto the cards. Leave some areas of white to draw in some detail.

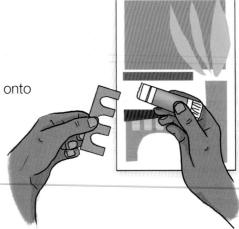

Make a cool COLLAGE!

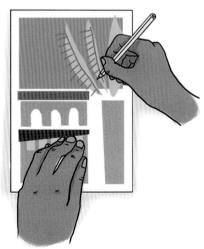

4 With some colored pencils, draw some details or patterns over the top of your collage. You could add some leaves on a tree, bricks on a building, or ripples in water. Write your message on the back, add a postage stamp, and go to the mail box!

New Baby Card  😊 ◯ ◯

Welcome a new baby with this colorful card, using stripes of pastel ribbons and bows. You can use traditional colors of blue for boys and pink for girls, or mix up the colors for something fun and eye-catching.

You will need

Pencil, scissors, and ruler

Thin card in blue or pink and white

Selection of ribbons

White (PVA) craft glue

1 Cut out a rectangle of colored card 6¼ x 6 in. (16 x 15 cm). Cut lengths of ribbon about 7 in. (18 cm) long. You will need between eight and ten pieces to cover your card.

2 Lay the strips of ribbon over the card, moving them around until you are happy with the arrangement. The ribbons should overhang the card by about ½ in. (1.5 cm) at each end. Trickle a line of glue along the ribbon but, to save mess, don't put glue on the overhanging ends yet. Stick the ribbons onto the card. making sure that they are straight.

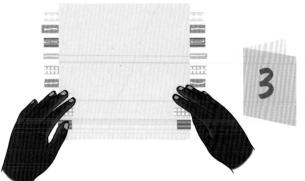

3 Turn the card over and glue the ends of the ribbons to the back, making sure that they are well stuck down.

BLUE for a BOY and PINK for a GIRL

4 Cut out a rectangle of white card 12½ x 7 in. (32 x 18 cm). Score down the center of the card and fold in half. Apply glue to the back of the ribbon card and stick it centrally onto the folded card.

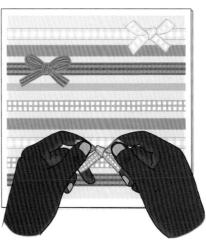

Tip

When sticking the ribbons in place, space them with different-sized gaps between the stripes to make the card look even more professional.

5 Choose three ribbons that have been used on the card and cut an 8-in. (20-cm) length of each. Tie them into bows (see page 13) and glue them onto the matching ribbon on the card.

Doily Valentine's Card ●○○

This pretty card uses a cake doily as a stencil to make a delicate lacy design. It will make a perfect Valentine's card when painted in white on pink or red card. Use other colors for a set of everyday notelets or unusual party invites.

You will need

Paper doilies

Scissors

Card blank

Masking tape

Paint

Saucer to hold paint

Fat paintbrush or stencil brush

Paper towel

Felt flowers (or hearts for Valentine's day)

White (PVA) craft glue

1 Cut a piece of doily a little larger than your card blank and attach it to the card with very small pieces of masking tape.

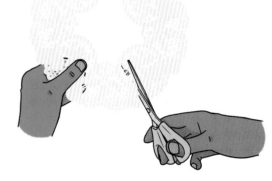

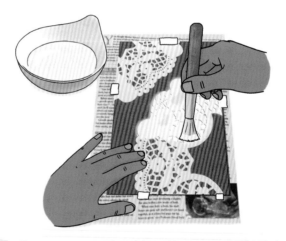

Lovely LACE

2 Cover your work table with some newspaper to protect it. Pour a little paint onto a saucer and dip the brush in the paint. Wipe the brush on a piece of paper towel to dry it a little—it needs to be quite dry so the paint doesn't spread. Now hold the brush upright and dab the whole doily with paint so every gap is filled. If you want to see the edge of the doily you will have to paint over the edge. Do this lightly, keeping an upright brush for a speckly effect.

3 Let the paint dry slightly for a few minutes, then carefully peel off the masking tape and gently lift the doily stencil off the card to reveal the lacy design.

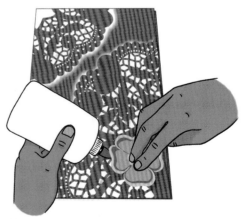

4 Let the paint dry completely and then finish the card by gluing a small felt flower or heart to the front.

Wedding Cake Card ☺○○

The wedding cake on this card, made with pretty papers, tiny pearl buttons, and shiny braid, looks almost as good as the real thing! Choose colors of paper and braid that work together, either using soft shades of silver and gray, or something bright and funky.

You will need

Templates on page109

Pencil, scissors, and ruler

Thin card in cream and gray

Silver paper

Five different patterned papers, (handmade paper looks lovely)

Glue stick

Selection of silver braids and small buttons or sequins

White (PVA) craft glue

Ribbon for bow

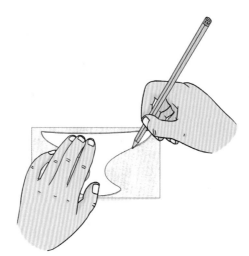

1 Cut out a rectangle of gray card measuring 8¼ x 5¾ in. (21 x 14.5 cm). Copy the templates from page 109 and cut out. Draw around the cake stand shape on silver paper, cut out with scissors, and glue onto the gray card with glue stick.

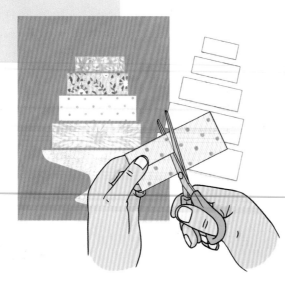

2 Using the templates, cut out the cake layers, using a different paper for each one. Arrange these above the cake stand on the card background and glue in place with glue stick.

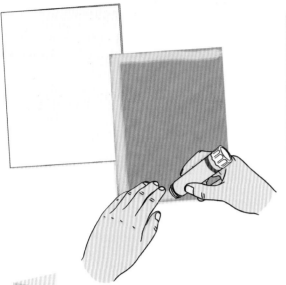

3 Cut out a rectangle of cream card measuring 8¾ x 12½ in. (22.5 x 32 cm). Score down the center and fold in half. Glue the decorated card to the front of the card using glue stick.

4 Cut lengths of braid to the same width as the lower edge of each cake tier. Arrange them, adding small buttons or other decorations, if you like. When you are happy with the positioning, glue them in place using craft glue. Add a small bow to the cake stand, gluing it firmly in place.

Here comes the BRIDE!

Templates

All the templates for the projects are included here, either at full size (100%) so that you can simply trace them (see page 9) or photocopy them, or at half the proper size (50%)—this means you need to ask an adult to help you to photocopy the template at double the size, using the 200% zoom button on the photocopier.

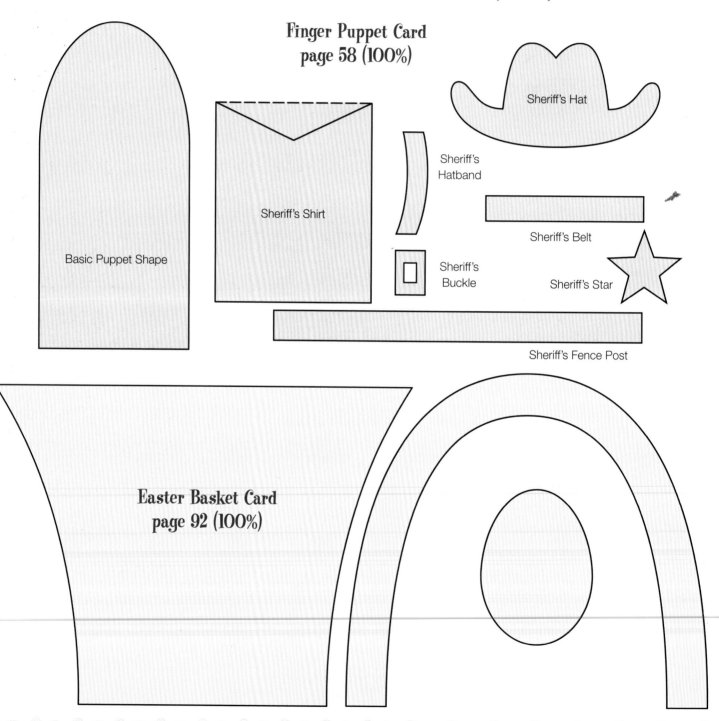

**Finger Puppet Card
page 58 (100%)**

Sheriff's Hat

Sheriff's Hatband

Sheriff's Belt

Basic Puppet Shape

Sheriff's Shirt

Sheriff's Buckle

Sheriff's Star

Sheriff's Fence Post

**Easter Basket Card
page 92 (100%)**

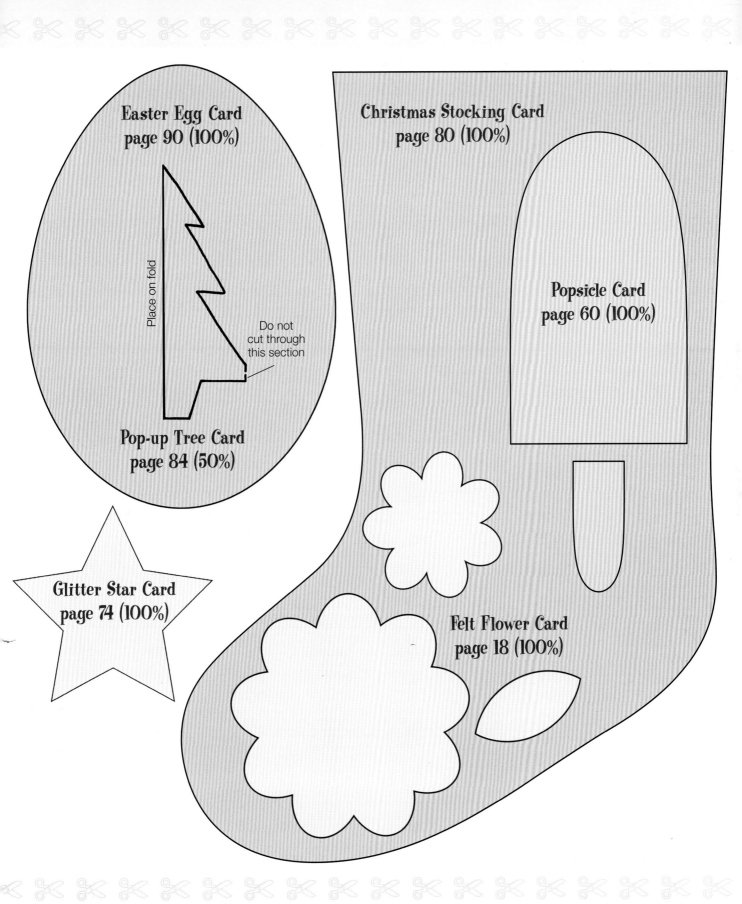

Easter Egg Card
page 90 (100%)

Place on fold

Do not
cut through
this section

Pop-up Tree Card
page 84 (50%)

Christmas Stocking Card
page 80 (100%)

Popsicle Card
page 60 (100%)

Glitter Star Card
page 74 (100%)

Felt Flower Card
page 18 (100%)

Ribbon Bouquet Card
page 30 (100%)

Russian Doll Card
page 64 (100%)

Flower Fairy Card
page 32 (100%)

Patchwork Card
page 44 (100%)

Patchwork Card
page 44 (100%)

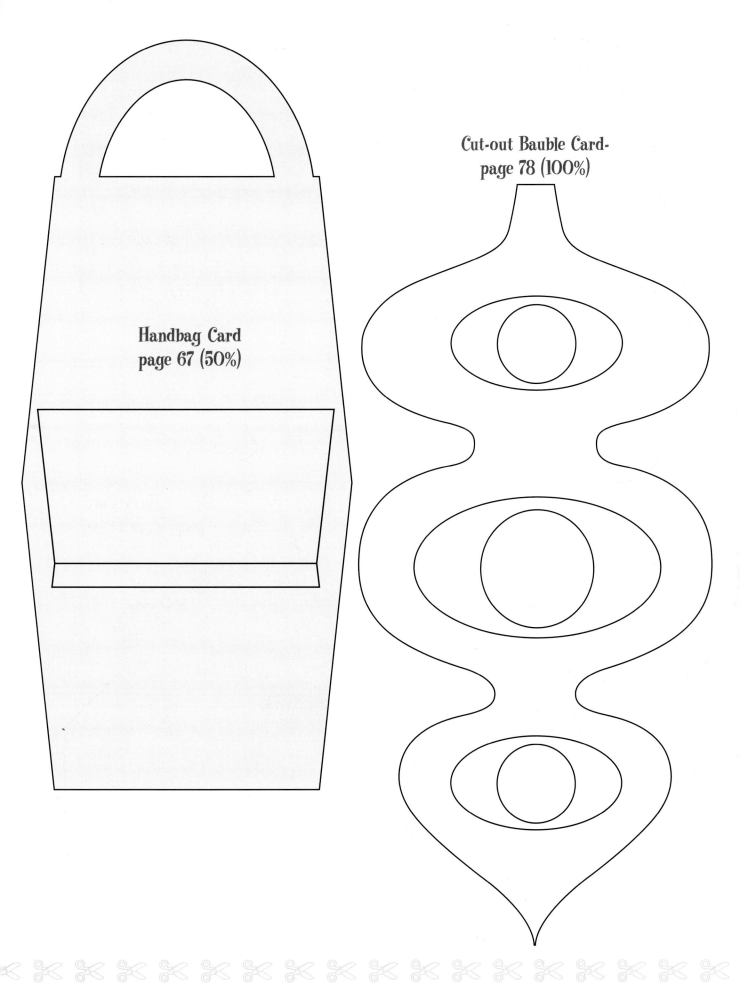

Handbag Card
page 67 (50%)

Cut-out Bauble Card-
page 78 (100%)

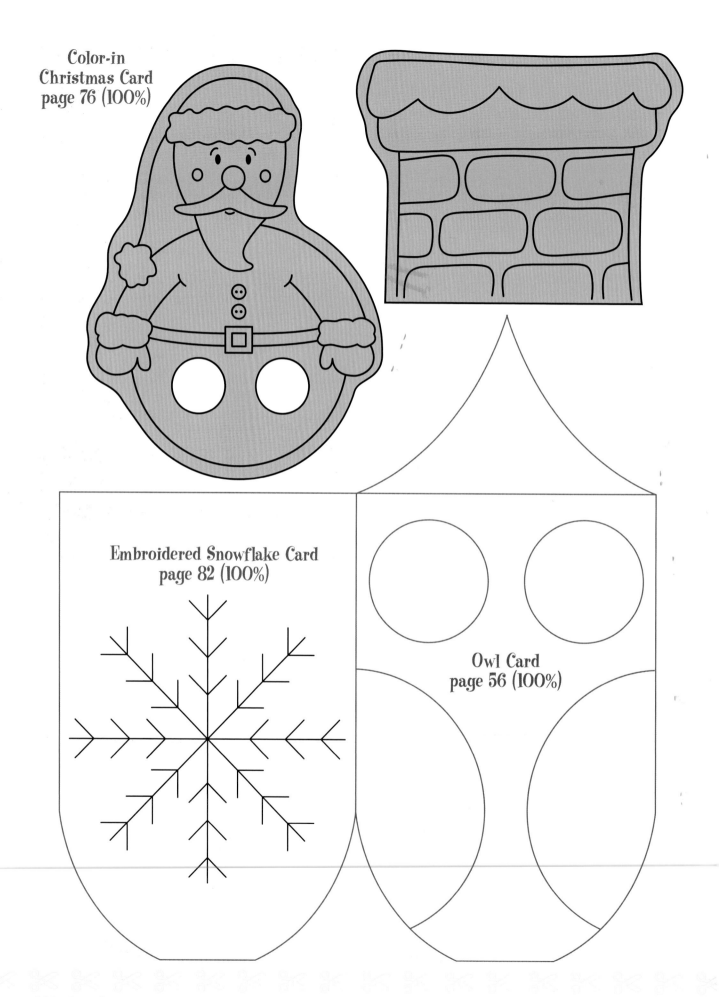

Color-in
Christmas Card
page 76 (100%)

Embroidered Snowflake Card
page 82 (100%)

Owl Card
page 56 (100%)

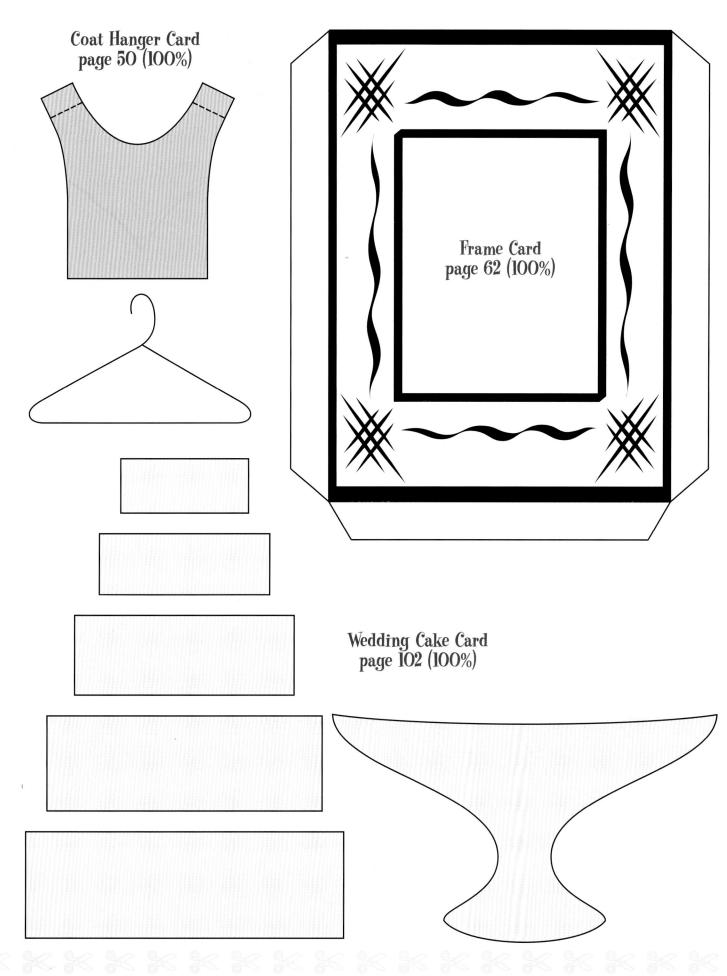

Coat Hanger Card
page 50 (100%)

Frame Card
page 62 (100%)

Wedding Cake Card
page 102 (100%)

Button Nest Card
page 38 (100%)

Raffia Card
page 40 (100%)

Fold-out Petal Card
page 35 (100%)

Mini Bunting Card
page 53 (100%)

Suppliers

Index

US

A C Moore
www.acmoore.com

Create for Less
www.createforless.com

The Cookie Cutter Company
www.cookiecuttercompany.com

Darice
www.darice.com

Hobby Lobby
www.hobbylobby.com

Jo-ann Fabric & Crafts
www.joann.com

Michaels
www.michaels.com

Mister Art
www.misterart.com

Walmart
www.walmart.com

UK

Baker Ross
www.bakerross.co.uk

Cakes, Cookies and Crafts
www.cakescookiesand
craftsshop.co.uk

Early Learning Centre
www.elc.co.uk

Homecrafts
www.homecrafts.co.uk

Hobbycraft
www.hobbycraft.co.uk

John Lewis
www.johnlewis.com

Lakeland
www.lakeland.co.uk

Mulberry Bush
www.mulberrybush.co.uk

The Works
www.theworks.co.uk

Yellow Moon
www.yellowmoon.org.uk

Credits

Project Makers

Libby Abadee and Cath Armstrong: Op Art p.28,
  Color-in Christmas Card p.76
Emma Hardy: Felt Flower Card p.18, Blossom
  Hole-punch Card p.20, Flower Stamp Card
  p.26, Ribbon Bouquet Card p. 30, Flower Fairy
  Card p.32, Raffia Card p.40, Wallpaper Notelet
  p. 42, Rosette Card p.48, Coat Hanger Card
  p.50, Finger Puppet Card p.58, Popsicle Card
  p.60, Handbag Card p.67, Glitter Star Card
  p.74, Christmas Stocking Card p.80, Easter Egg
  Card p.90, Easter Basket Card p.92, New Baby
  Card p.98, Wedding Cake Card p.102
Clare Youngs: Fold-out Petal Card p.35, Button
  Nest Card p.38, Patchwork Card p.44, Mini
  Bunting Card p.53, Owl Card p.56, Russian
  Doll Card p.64, Fingerprint Pups p.70, Cut-out
  Bauble card p.78, Picasso Postcard p.96
Catherine Woram: Cross-stitch Card p.23,
  Embroidered Snowflake Card p.82, Pop-up Tree
  Card p.84, Doily Valentine's Card p.100

Photography Credits

Caroline Arber: pp. 71, 72, 83, 97
Cath Armstrong: pp.29, 77
James Gardiner and Claire Richardson: pp. 45, 73
  top right, 79
Jacqui Hurst: pp. 2, 3, 11, 13, 16, 19, 21, 27, 31,
  41, 43, 46, 47 top left, 49, 51, 59, 61, 63,
  67–69, 73 bottom left, 75, 81, 86, 87 bottom
  right, 91, 93, 99, 103
Debbie Patterson: pp. 17 top right, 33
Claire Richardson: pp. 1, 3, 4-5, 6, 17 bottom
  left, 35, 37, 39, 47 bottom right, 53, 55,
  57, 65

Polly Wreford: pp. 7, 85, 87 top left, 89, 101
Penny Wincer: 23, 24